Contents

English
Paper Money

BY VINCENT DUGGLEBY

The above work will give you the further
specialised information which you may need.

It is a heavily illustrated hardback book of 120
pages available from Stanley Gibbons shops, postal
sales department or your usual supplier. Price £3.50.

Collect
British
Banknotes

A Stanley Gibbons Priced Catalogue
of British Treasury and
Bank of England Notes

SECOND EDITION

Stanley Gibbons Publications Ltd
391 Strand, London WC2R 0LX

By Appointment
to H.M. the Queen,
Philatelists

By Appointment to Her Majesty The Queen
Stanley Gibbons Ltd, Philatelists

© Stanley Gibbons Publications Ltd, 1977
First published 1970
Second edition 1977

This edition is a condensation of Vincent Duggleby's
English Paper Money prepared by James Negus

ISSN 0309 – 5673
ISBN 0 85259 960 9

Printed in Great Britain by Colmore Press Ltd

Introduction

In Britain the new collector of English paper money will find that he can make a good start by examining the banknotes in his wallet. Apart from various denominations there are likely to be several different signatures. Check to see if the banknotes are misprints; sometimes the serial numbers on each note do not match. Make sure the prefix coding is normal: there are scarce prefix codings which add substantially to the value. They are listed in this catalogue.

O'Brien signature £1 notes are occasionally found in circulation. Check the backs to see if a little "R" occupies the space above the framed "Bank of England" on the lower left side: it is a rarity. "G" notes are worth looking for too; the letter is in the same position on Hollom and Fforde notes as the "R" on O'Brien notes, but they are found more frequently.

Vincent Duggleby, well known from the BBC programme "The Financial World Tonight", is recognised as the leading authority on modern British Treasury and Bank of England notes of the twentieth century. In 1975 Stanley Gibbons published his hardback book *English Paper Money,* based on much original research and containing full information and numerous illustrations of these issues.

The specialist collector and dealer will find Mr. Duggleby's book essential and it is currently available, price £3.50. It was felt, however, that a condensed version would also be of use to the many new and existing collectors who need a quick guide, without too much detail, to what modern notes exist. A format suitable for carrying in the pocket was also considered helpful.

The same catalogue numbers as were used in Mr. Duggleby's book have been retained here. Where later information has become available, the original text has been corrected, however.

Prices

Banknotes have been priced for Very Fine (VF) and Extremely Fine (EF) conditions. It should be remembered that many of them can be obtained for very much less in worn condition; 100% uncirculated notes cost more. The abbreviation *ea* means "each".

In the price columns a dagger (†) means that the note is readily obtained from circulation. The present catalogue has updated prices, correct at the time of going to press.

JAMES NEGUS

Catalogue Terms

OBVERSE: Front of a banknote.

REVERSE: Back of a banknote.

PREFIX: The combination of letters and numbers preceding the serial number.

DOT: A full stop after or under the "o" in "No."

DASH: As above, but a dash instead of a full stop. Also known as "square dot".

THREAD: A metal filament or thread inserted into the paper, clearly visible when the note is held up to the light.

Most illustrations are approximately half-linear; the high-value black and white notes of Mahon to O'Brien are, however, reproduced about 40% linear.

Illustrations of prefixes are not reproduced from actual notes but are shown in similar typefaces purely for identification.

Price quotations are in pounds sterling throughout.

EARLY BANK OF ENGLAND
NOTES

The story of the Bank of England is told in Vincent Duggleby's book *English Paper Money* and a full priced catalogue is included there for the many fascinating (and rare) notes issued from the date of the Bank's founding in 1694.

Up to 1725 notes had hand-written amounts, although part printing with a Britannia medallion had been introduced about 1696. Between 1725 and 1745 notes were printed in denominations of "round" figures (£20 up to £1000) and odd amounts could be added in handwriting. Between 1759 and the end of the eighteenth century notes were introduced with the word "pound(s)" printed after the figures, so that handwritten additions to value gradually lapsed.

All following series of notes, up to the modern era beginning 1928, are classified according to the payee. This is either:

The Chief Cashier of the Bank
or The Bearer on Demand.

The Chief Cashier was shown as payee often from 1752 and always from 1782 to 1855. Originally handwritten, but from 1798 printed, the names were:

Abraham Newland	1782-1807
Henry Hase	1807-29
Thomas Rippon	1829-35
Matthew Marshall	1835-55

Denominations ranged from £1 to £1000.

The familiar words "I promise to pay the bearer on demand" appear as payee from 1855. The Chief Cashier's signature is now shown only as a watermark in the paper, as follows:

Matthew Marshall	1855-64
William Miller	1864-66
George Forbes	1866-70

Denominations were £5 to £1000. Various members of the Bank staff signed the notes by hand.

The last phase occurs from 1870 when the printed signature of the Chief Cashier appears on all notes. The names found are:

George Forbes	1870-73
F. May	1873-93
H. G. Bowen	1893-1902
John Gordon Nairne	1902-18
Ernest Musgrave Harvey	1918-25

Denominations are £5 to £1000 again. As is well known, the denomination £1 was covered by a coin, the famous "Golden Sovereign." There was also a half-sovereign coin for 10 shillings (our present 50p).

From 1826 until 1925 notes can be found with the name of a branch bank, instead of London, printed on them. They are worth from twice as much as a corresponding normal "London" note. Names of Branches which occur are:

Birmingham	Liverpool
Bristol	Manchester
Exeter	Newcastle
Gloucester	Norwich
Hull	Plymouth
Leeds	Portsmouth
Leicester	Swansea

With the outbreak of War in 1914 the Government fully expected the gold coins to be hoarded. Bank of England notes at the time were legal tender in England and Wales only for amounts of £5 and over. Legislation was hurriedly passed to allow the Treasury to issue currency notes of full legal tender and this they continued to do up to 1928 (their notes were withdrawn in 1933). A priced catalogue of these Treasury issues begins at page 3.

Though the Treasury was the organisation chosen to fill the gap with notes below £5 the Bank of England had, nevertheless, been making their own preparations in the summer of 1914. One of the most exciting British notes dates from this time, the so-called "Nairne" £1. This is a banknote, known only as a proof and never issued, signed by J. G. Nairne as Chief Cashier. Only four copies are known and one fetched £1200 when auctioned by Stanley Gibbons Currency Ltd in 1975.

The Bank of England was once again given authority to print and issue currency notes in 1928. It produced a 10s. note for the first time and reintroduced the £1 after a gap of over 100 years. A full priced catalogue is given beginning at page 15.

TREASURY NOTES

SIGNATURE JOHN BRADBURY

First Issue

Prefix T1

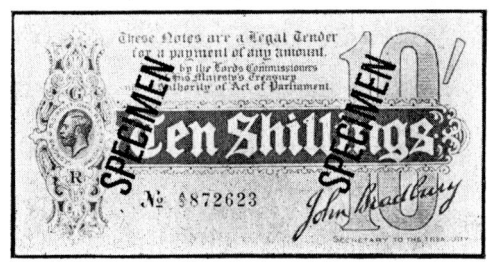

Prefix T9

*Both notes are printed on one
side only*

3

A 754774 $^{S}_{32}$ № 062350

T2   T3

$^{J}_{20}$№ 75530 $^{K}_{20}$№ 39217

T4   T5

$^{DD}_{26}$№ 012471 $^{D}_{18}$№ 003659

T6   T7

The seven types of the £1 are distinguished by prefixes and serial
numbers (*see* diagram and banknote on page 3):

	Prefix	*No.*	*Serial-number digits*
T1	Large capital letter & full stop	—	Six
T2	Large capital letter, no full stop	—	Six
T3	Letter over number	With dot	Six
T4	Letter over number	With dot	Five
T5	Letter over number	With dash	Five
T6	Double letter over number	With dot	Six
T7	Letter over number	With dash	Six

T7 is in a smaller typeface than T3.

1914	**£1 black on white**		EF	VF
T1	Serial letter	A	£145	85·00
		B	£130	70·00
		C	£150	90·00
T2	Serial letter	A	£145	85·00
		B	£130	70·00
		C	£150	90·00
T3			£120	60·00
T4			£125	65·00
T5			£130	70·00
T6			£130	70·00
T7			£140	80·00

4

$^{D}_{25}$ № 747283 $^{B}_{71}$ № 32557

T8   T10

10s. red on white

T8	Six digits	£140	80·00
T9	Six digits; No. precedes prefix	£130	70·00
	(*see* banknote illustrated on page 3)		
T10	Five digits	£135	70·00

Notes T1—T10 are watermarked Royal Cypher and "POSTAGE".

For watermark sideways: add 25%.
For watermark inverted: add 50%.
For watermark sideways inverted: add 50%.

Second Issue

Wording "United Kingdom of Great Britain and Ireland"

*Both notes are printed on one
side only*

1914			EF	VF
T11	**£1 black on white**		65·00	35·00

1915			EF	VF
T12	**10s. red on white.**	Five digits	60·00	30·00
T13	**10s. red on white.**	Six digits	55·00	30·00
T14	**£1 black on white** overprinted in red in Arabic "Piastres silver 120"		*from* £1250	*from* £850
T15	**10s. red on white** overprinted in black in Arabic "Piastres silver 60"		£175	85·00

T14 and T15 were prepared for British
Forces in the Dardanelles Campaign.

Third Issue

Wording "United Kingdom of Great Britain and Ireland"

obverse
St. George and
Dragon

reverse
Houses of
Parliament

1917		EF	VF
T16	**£1 brown, purple and green on white or cream**		
	Prefix: letter over number		
	A	25·00	12·00
	B to H	ea 22·00	10·00
	Z	25·00	12·00

obverse
Britannia

reverse
Medallion

	N<u>O</u> dot	N<u>O</u> dash

1918

10s. green, purple and brown

T17	Serial in black; "dot" in No.	90·00	50·00
T18	Serial in black; "dash" in No.	80·00	45·00
T19	Serial in red; "dot" in No.	85·00	45·00
T20	Serial in red; "dash" in No.	75·00	40·00

A 5s. note was prepared in 1917 but not issued. Proofs are known of notes for 1s. and 2s. 6d. prepared in 1918.

SIGNATURE N. F. WARREN FISHER

obverse
St. George and
Dragon

9

reverse
Houses of
Parliament

1919

		EF	VF
T24	**£1 brown and green on white or cream**		

Prefix: letter over number

	EF	VF
K to P	*ca* 18·00	9·00
R to U	*ca* 18·00	9·00
W to Y	*ca* 18·00	9·00
Z	20·00	8·00

obverse
Britannia

reverse
Medallion

N°.	**N°**
dot	dash

10s. green, purple and brown

T25	"Dot" in No.	40·00	20·00
T26	"Dash" in No.	35·00	15·00

Notes for 1s., 2s. 6d. and 5s. were prepared in 1919 but not issued.

1922

10s. green, purple and brown

T30	"No." omitted	25·00	8·00

1923   EF   VF

New composite watermark with ONE POUND appearing at top.

£1 brown and green. Prefix: letter and figure "1" over number

T31	"Dot" in No.			
	A1	*ea*	18·00	8·00
	Z1		18·00	6·00
	Other letters	*ea*	16·00	6·00
T32	"Dash" in No.			
	All letters	*ea*	30·00	15·00

Fourth Issue

Wording altered to "United Kingdom of Great Britain and Northern Ireland

obverse
Britannia

reverse
Medallion

1927

T33   **10s. green, purple and brown**   30·00   15·00

obverse
St. George and
Dragon

reverse
Houses of
Parliament

dot   dash

	£1 brown and green. Prefix: letter and figure "1" over number			
T34	S1 to U1; "dot" in No.	*ea*	25·00	12·00
	W1 to Y1; "dot" in No.	*ea*	25·00	12·00
	Z1; "dot" in No.		27·00	14·00
T35	All letters; "dash" in No.	*ea*	30·00	15·00

Using the Catalogue
pages 15 – 55

1. Find the appropriate section of the catalogue from the signature on the note.

2. Identify the note from the denomination and illustrations.

3. In the list (following the illustration) check that the prefix's letter and number sequence given next to the denomination corresponds with the note.

4. The known prefix letters are then listed and each priced as EF (first column) and VF (second column).

Note. The " B " numbers are the catalogue numbers taken from Vincent Duggleby's *English Paper Money.* As the more specialised items listed in that book are omitted from the present catalogue, there are gaps in the sequence.

Where no date of issue is given for a particular note look back in the list where it will be found as referring to blocks of succeeding numbers.

MODERN BANK OF ENGLAND NOTES

In this section prefixes are abbreviated:
"L" means "Letter"
"No." means "Number"

SIGNATURE C. P. MAHON
Chief Cashier 1925-29

B210 obverse
Britannia medallion

B210 reverse
Scroll patterns

1928								EF	VF
B210	**10s. red-brown** L No. No.								
A01	..	..	..	..	..	..	..	75·00	40·00
V	..	..	..	..	..	..	..	50·00	20·00
W to Y	..	..	..	..	..	.. *ea*	25·00	8·00
Z	..	..	..	..	..	..	..	35·00	15·00

B212 obverse
Britannia medallion

B212 reverse
Bank of England

1928							EF	VF
B212	**£1 green**	L No. No.						
	A01 ..	..	..	..	..	..	75·00	40·00
	Other A ..	..	..	..	..	..	25·00	10·00
	B to G	..	..	..	..	.. ea	22·00	7·00
	H	..	..	..	..	..	40·00	15·00

Design for £5 to £1000

1925	(and dates up to 1929)				EF	VF
B215	**£5 black on white**	..	..	..	30·00	15·00
B216	**£10 black on white** ..	..	..	..	45·00	20·00
B217	**£20 black on white** ..	..	..	..	75·00	40·00
B218	**£50 black on white** ..	..	..	from	£200	
B219	**£100 black on white**	..	..	from	£350	
B220	**£200 black on white**	..	..	from	£2000	
B221	**£500 black on white**	..	..	from	£3000	
B222	**£1000 black on white**	..	..	from	£4000	

Premium for branch notes: from 15%.

SIGNATURE B. G. CATTERNS
Chief Cashier 1929-34

B223 obverse
Britannia medallion

B223 reverse
Scroll patterns

1930								EF	VF
B223	**10s. red-brown**	L No. No.							
K	..	..	..	..	..	..	..	22·00	8·00
L to O	..	..	..	..	..	..	*ea*	20·00	7·00
R to U	..	..	..	..	..	..	*ea*	20·00	7·00
V	..	..	..	..	..	..	..	25·00	9·00

Plate 2 notes (design 128mm wide) are worth 20% more than the plate 1 notes above (126mm wide).

B225 obverse
Britannia medallion

B225/6 reverse
Bank of England

	1930								EF	VF
B225	**£1 green**	L No. No.								
	H	..	..	..	..	..	..	..	22·00	10·00
	J to O	..	..	..	..	..	.. *ea*	15·00	6·00
	R to U	..	..	..	..	..	.. *ea*	15·00	6·00
	W to Y	..	..	..	..	..	.. *ea*	15·00	6·00
	Z	..	..	..	..	..	..	..	17·00	6·50
B226	**£1 green**	No. No. L								
	A	..	..	..	..	..	..	..	28·00	12·00

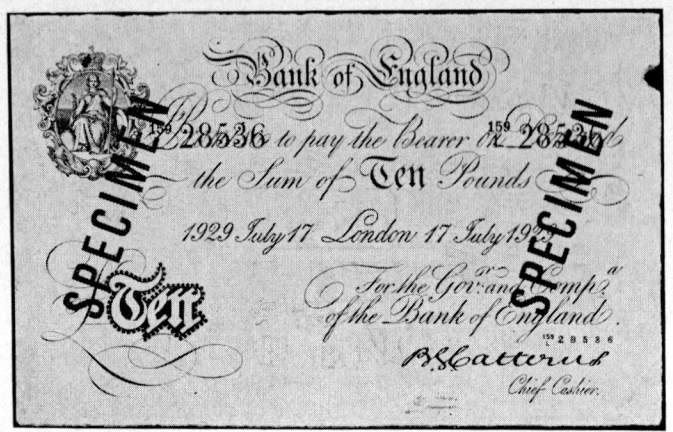

Design for £5 to £1000

1929	(and dates up to 1934)				EF	VF
B228	**£5 black on white**	..	..	..	30·00	15·00
B229	**£10 black on white** ..	..	..	..	45·00	20·00
B230	**£20 black on white** ..	..	..	..	75·00	40·00
B231	**£50 black on white** ..	..	..	*from* £200	
B232	**£100 black on white**	..	..	*from* £350	
B233	**£500 black on white**	..	..	*from* £3000	
B234	**£1000 black on white**	..	..	*from* £4000	

Premium for branch notes: from 15%.

SIGNATURE K. O. PEPPIATT
Chief Cashier 1934-49
First Period (1934-39)

B236 obverse
Britannia medallion

B235/6 reverse
Scroll patterns

1934

B235	**10s. red-brown** L No. No.							EF	VF
A	..	..	..	..	..	..	..	20·00	5·00
B to D	..	..	..	..	..	.. *ea*	16·00	3·50
E	..	..	..	..	..	..	..	16·00	3·50
H	..	..	..	..	..	..	..	16·00	3·50
J	..	..	..	..	..	..	..	18·00	5·00

Plate 2 notes (design 128mm wide) are worth 25% more than the plate 1 notes above (126mm wide).

B236 **10s. red-brown**   No. No. L

O	..	..	..	..	..	..	..	14·00	4·00
R to U	..	..	..	..	..	.. *ea*	12·00	3·50
W to Y	..	..	..	..	..	.. *ea*	12·00	3·50
Z	..	..	..	..	..	..	..	14·00	4·00

Plate 2 notes (design 128mm wide) are worth 10% more than the plate 1 notes above (126mm wide). *See also* B256.

B238 obverse
Britannia medallion

B238/9 reverse
Bank of England

B238	**£1 green**	No. No. L									
	B	..	..	..	..	..	..	..		12·00	4·00
	C to E	..	..	..	..	..	..	ea	10·00	3·00
	H	..	..	..	..	..	..	..	10·00	3·00
	J to O	..	..	..	..	..	..	ea	10·00	3·00
	R to U	..	..	..	..	..	..	ea	10·00	3·00
	W to Y	..	..	..	..	..	..	ea	10·00	3·00
	Z	..	..	..	..	..	..	..	10·00	3·00

B239	**£1 green**	L No. No. L									
	A — A	..	..	..	..	..	..		12·00	4·00
	B — A to E — A	..	..	..	..	ea	10·00	3·00
	H — A	..	..	..	..	..	..	10·00	3·00
	J — A	..	..	..	..	..	..	10·00	3·00
	K — A	..	..	..	..	..	..	10·00	3·00
	L — A	..	..	..	..	..	..	11·00	3·50

See also B258.

Design for £5 to £1000

1934	(and dates up to 1943)					EF	VF
B241	**£5 black on white**	..	..	..	..	25·00	15·00
B242	**£10 black on white**	..	..	..	..	45·00	20·00
B243	**£20 black on white**	..	..	..	..	75·00	40·00
B244	**£50 black on white**	..	..	*from*	£200		
B245	**£100 black on white**	..	..	*from*	£350		
B246	**£500 black on white**	..	..	*from*	£3000		
B247	**£1000 black on white**	..	..	*from*	£4000		

Premium for branch notes: from 15%.

Second Period (1940-48)

Metal thread incorporated (all denominations). Colours of 10s. and £1 changed. On £1 obverse a double line around watermark area (single line hitherto).

1940							EF	VF
B248	**£1 pale blue**	L No. No. L						
	A — D	..	..	..	..	..	..	12·00	4·00
	A — E	..	..	..	..	..	..	7·50	2·50
	A — H	..	..	..	..	..	..	7·50	2·50
B249	**£1 blue**	L No. No. L						
	B — D to E — D	..	..	..	.. *ea*	4·50	2·00
	H — D	..	..	..	..	..	4·50	2·00
	J — D to O — D	..	..	..	.. *ea*	4·50	2·00
	R — D to U — D	..	..	..	.. *ea*	4·50	2·00
	W — D to Y — D	..	..	..	.. *ea*	4·50	2·00
	Z — D	..	..	..	..	..	6·00	3·00
	B — E to E — E	..	..	..	.. *ea*	4·50	2·00
	H — E	..	..	..	..	..	4·50	2·00
	J — E to O — E	..	..	..	.. *ea*	4·50	2·00
	R — E to U — E	..	..	..	.. *ea*	4·50	2·00
	W — E	..	..	..	..	..	4·50	2·00
	B — H to E — H	..	..	..	.. *ea*	4·50	2·00
	H — H	..	..	..	..	..	4·50	2·00
	J — H to O — H	..	..	..	.. *ea*	4·50	2·00
	R — H to U — H	..	..	..	.. *ea*	4·50	2·00
	W — H or X — H	..	..	..	.. *ea*	4·50	2·00

B251 **10s. mauve** L No. No. L

A — D	..	..	..	..	..	..		7·50	2·50
B — D to E — D	..	..	..	.. ea	6·00	2·00
H — D	..	..	..	..	..	..		6·00	2·00
J — D to O — D	..	..	..	.. ea	6·00	2·00
R — D to U — D	..	..	..	.. ea	6·00	2·00
W — D to Y — D	..	..	..	.. ea	6·00	2·00
Z — D	..	..	..	..	..		7·50	2·50

X — E	..	..	..	..	..	..	7·50	2·00
Y — E	..	..	..	..	..	..	6·00	2·00
Z — E	..	..	..	..	..	..	7·50	2·00

1944-45   EF   VF

B255 **£5 black on white** L No. No.

E	..	..	..	..	..	..	..	20·00	12·00
H	..	..	..	..	..	..	..	20·00	12·00
J or K	..	..	..	..	..	..	20·00	12·00

Third Period (1948)

Unthreaded 10s. and £1 notes of Peppiatt First Period issued from stockpiles. Distinguish by serial letters.

1948   EF   VF

B256 **10s. red-brown** No. No. L

L	..	..	..	..	..	..	..	15·00	8·00

B258 **£1 green** L No. No. L

R — A	..	..	..	..	..	..	12·00	5·00
S — A	..	..	..	..	..	..	15·00	5·00

Fourth Period (1948-49)

Metal thread incorporated (all denominations).

1948   EF   VF

B260 **£1 green** L No. No. L

A — B	..	..	..	..	..	..	8·00	3·00
B — B to E — B	..	..	..	.. ea	7·00	3·00
H — B	..	..	..	..	..	..	11·00	4·00

S — A		12·00	4·00
T — A or U — A .. .. *ea*		7·00	3·00
W — A to Y — A .. .. *ea*		7·00	3·00
Z — A		9·00	3·50

Prices are for plate 1 (width of design 141·5mm).

Add 20% for the larger plates 2 or 3.

B262 **10s. red-brown** No. No. L
— E, — H, — J or — K .. .. .. *ea* 12·00		4·00
— L .. .. 22·00		12·00

Prices are for plate 2 (width of design 129mm).

Add 25% for plate 1 (126mm) or 50% for plate 3 (131mm).

B264 **£5 black on white** L No. No.

As B255 but on thin paper. All notes dated 1947.

— L or — M .. .. 25·00   12·00

SIGNATURE P. S. BEALE

Chief Cashier 1949-55

B265 obverse
Britannia medallion

26

B265/6 reverse
Scroll patterns

1950

			EF	VF
B265	**10s. red-brown** No. No. L			
	— B to — D .. .. *ea*		9·00	4·00
	— E		25·00	10·00
B266	**10s. red-brown** L No. No. L			
	D — Z		8·50	3·00
	E — Z		5·50	2·50
	H — Z		5·50	2·50
	J — Z to O — Z .. .. *ea*		5·50	2·50
	R — Z to U — Z .. .. *ea*		5·50	2·50
	W — Z to Y — Z .. .. *ea*		5·50	2·50
	Z — Z		8·50	3·00

B268 obverse
Britannia medallion

27

B268 reverse
Bank of England

B268 **£1 green** L No. No. L

H — B	..	..	..	..	..	9·00	3·50
J — B to O — B	..	..	..	.. *ea*	4·50	2·00
R — B to U — B	..	..	..	.. *ea*	4·50	2·00
W — B to Y — B	..	..	..	.. *ea*	4·50	2·00
Z — B	..	..	..	..	5·00	2·50
A — C	..	..	..	..	5·00	2·50
B — C to E — C	..	..	..	.. *ea*	4·50	2·00
H — C	..	..	..	..	4·50	2·00
J — C to O — C	..	..	..	.. *ea*	4·50	2·00
R — C to U — C	..	..	..	.. *ea*	4·50	2·00
W — C to Y — C	..	..	..	.. *ea*	4·50	2·00
Z — C	..	..	..	..	5·00	2·50
A — J	..	..	..	..	5·00	2·50
B — J to E — J	..	..	..	.. *ea*	4·50	2·00
H — J	..	..	..	..	4·50	2·00
J — J or K — J	..	..	..	..	4·50	2·00
L — J	..	..	..	..	9·00	3·50

28

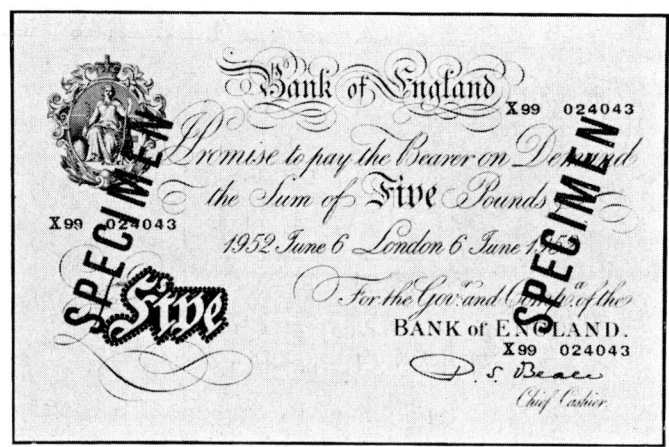

1949			EF	VF
B270	**£5 black on white** L No. No.			
	M — to P — ..	.. ..	18·00	10·00
	R — to Y — ..	.. ..	18·00	10·00

SIGNATURE L. K. O'BRIEN
Chief Cashier 1955-62
First (Britannia) Period (1955-60)

B271 obverse
Britannia medallion

29

B271 reverse
Scroll patterns

1955							EF	VF
B271 **10s. red-brown** L No. No. L								
Y — X or Z — X	..	..	..	..	*ea*	5·00	2·50
A — Y	..	..	..	..		5·00	2·50
B — Y to E — Y	..	..	..	..	*ea*	4·00	2·00
H — Y	..	..	..	..		4·00	2·00
J — Y to O — Y	..	..	..	..	*ea*	4·00	2·00
R — Y to U — Y	..	..	..	..	*ea*	4·00	2·00
W — Y to Y — Y	..	..	..	..	*ea*	4·00	2·00
Z — Y	..	..	..	..		5·00	2·50
A — Z	..	..	..	..		6·00	2·50
B — Z or C — Z	..	..	..	..		4·00	2·00
D — Z	..	..	..	..		9·00	4·00

B273 obverse
Britannia medallion

B273 reverse
Bank of England

B273 **£1 green** L No. No. L

L — J	..	..	..	..	..	..	8·00	3·50
M — J to O — J	..	..	..	.. *ea*	4·00	2·00
R — J to U — J	..	..	..	.. *ea*	4·00	2·00
W — J to Y — J	..	..	..	.. *ea*	4·00	2·00
Z — J	..	..	..	..	..	..	5·00	2·00

A — K	..	..	..	..	5·00	2·00
B — K to E — K	..	..	..	.. ea	4·00	2·00
H — K	..	..	..	..	4·00	2·00
J — K to O — K	..	..	..	.. ea	4·00	2·00
R — K to U — K	..	..	..	.. ea	4·00	2·00
W — K to Y — K	..	..	..	.. ea	4·00	2·00
Z — K	..	..	..	..	5·00	2·00
A — L	..	..	..	..	5·00	2·00
B — L to E — L	..	..	..	.. ea	4·00	2·00
H — L to J — L	..	..	..	.. ea	4·00	2·00
K — L	..	..	..	..	6·00	3·50

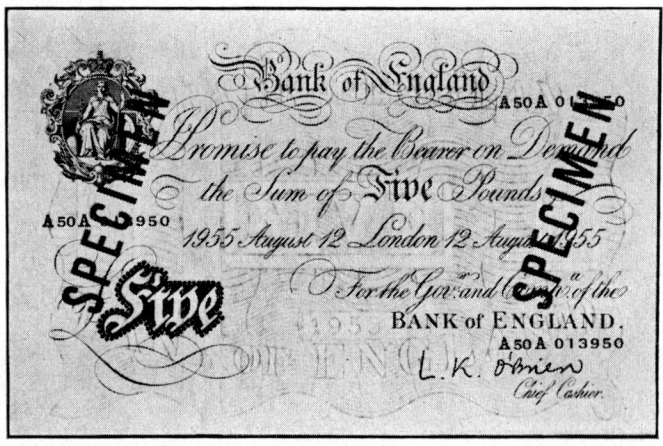

B275 **£5 black on white** L No. No.

Z —	20·00	10·00

B276 **£5 black on white** L No. No. L

A — A	20·00	10·00
B — A or C — A .. .. ea	18·00	9·00
D — A	20·00	10·00

B277/9 obverse
Helmeted Britannia

B277 reverse
Lion & key:
£5 symbols shaded

1957							EF	VF
B277	**£5 blue, pale green & orange**		L No. No.					
	A —	..	..	..	..	..	11·00	8·00
	B — to E —	..	..	..	..	.. *ea*	10·00	7·50
	H —	..	..	..	..	..	10·00	7·50

B279/80 reverse
Lion & key: £5 symbols
in outline only

1961			EF	VF
B279	**£5 blue, pale green & orange**	L No. No.		
	H —, J — or K — .. .. *ea*		10·00	7·50
B280	**£5 blue, pale green & orange**	L No. No.		
	M —		15·00	9·00

Second (Portrait) Period (1960-62)

B281 obverse
Queen's portrait

B281/2 reverse
Seated Britannia

1960   EF   VF

B281 **£1 green** L No. No.

A —   .. ..   5·00   2·50
B — to E — .. .. *ea* 4·00   2·00
H —   .. ..   4·00   2·00
J — to N — .. .. *ea* 4·00   2·00
R — to U — .. .. *ea* 4·00   2·00
W — to Y — .. .. *ea* 4·00   2·00
Z —   .. ..   5·00   2·50

B282 **£1 green** No. No. L

— A   .. ..   5·00   2·50
— B to — E .. .. *ea* 4·00   2·00
— H   .. ..   4·00   2·00
— J to — N .. .. *ea* 4·00   2·00
— R to — U .. .. *ea* 4·00   2·00
— W to — Y .. .. *ea* 4·00   2·00
— Z   .. ..   5·00   2·50

"R" Variety on reverse

B283 **£1 green** L No. No. L, with capital "R" on reverse
     A — N   .. ..   90·00 *from* 35·00
     The "R" distinguished an experimental printing from a
reel-fed machine.

B284 **£1 green** L No. No. L
     B — N   .. ..   12·00   4·00

B286 obverse
Queen's portrait

B286 reverse
Seated Britannia

1961   EF   VF

B286 **10s. red-brown** L No. No.

							EF	VF
A —	..	..	..	..	..	..	5·00	2·50
B — to E —	..	..	..	..	.. ea	4·00	2·00
H — or J —	..	..	..	..	.. ea	4·00	2·00
K —	..	..	..	..	..	..	5·00	2·50

SIGNATURE J. Q. HOLLOM

Chief Cashier 1962-66

B288 obverse
Queen's portrait

37

B288 reverse
Seated Britannia

1963								EF	VF
B288	**£1 green** L No. No. L								
	B — N	..	..	..	..	..	..	14·00	7·00
	C — N to E — N	..	..	..	*ea*	4·00	2·00		
	H — N	..	..	..	..	..	4·00	2·00	
	J — N to L — N	..	..	..	*ea*	4·00	2·00		
	A — R to E — R	..	..	..	*ea*	4·00	2·00		
	H — R	..	..	..	..	..	4·00	2·00	
	J — R to L — R	..	..	..	*ea*	4·00	2·00		
	A — S to E — S	..	..	..	*ea*	4·00	2·00		
	H — S	..	..	..	..	..	4·00	2·00	
	J — S to L — S	..	..	..	*ea*	4·00	2·00		
	A — T to C — T	..	..	..	*ea*	4·00	2·00		
	E — T	..	..	..	..	..	4·00	2·00	
	H — T	..	..	..	..	..	4·00	2·00	
	J — T to L — T	..	..	..	*ea*	4·00	2·00		
	A — U to E — U	..	..	..	*ea*	4·00	2·00		
	H — U	..	..	..	..	..	4·00	2·00	
	J — U to L — U	..	..	..	*ea*	4·00	2·00		
	A — W or B — W	..	..	..	*ea*	4·00	2·00		
	D — W or E — W	..	..	..	*ea*	4·00	2·00		
	H — W	..	..	..	..	..	4·00	2·00	
	J — W to L — W	..	..	..	*ea*	4·00	2·00		

A — X to E — X ..	..	..	..	*ea*	4·00	2·00
H — X to K — X ..	..	..	..	*ea*	4·00	2·00
A — Y ..	..	..	..	..	..	4·00	2·00
B — Y ..	..	..	..	..	..	10·00	4·00

"G" variety on reverse

B292 **£1 green**   L No. No. L, with capital "G" on reverse

A — N ..	..	..	..	..	..	8·50	3·50
D — T ..	..	..	..	..	..	6·00	3·00
C — W ..	..	..	..	..	..	6·00	3·00
L — X ..	..	..	..	..	..	6·00	3·00

The "G" identified printing on a Gobel machine.

B295 obverse
Queen's portrait

B294/5 reverse
Seated Britannia

B294 **10s. red-brown** L No. No.

K —		..	..	..	..	..	..	4·50	3·00
L —		..	..	..	..	..	..	3·00	2·00
N —		..	..	..	..	..	..	3·00	2·00
R — to U —	..	..	..	..	..	*ea*		3·00	2·00
W — to Y —	..	..	..	..	..	*ea*		3·00	2·00

B295 **10s. red-brown** No. No. L

— A		..	..	..	..	..	..	4·50	3·00
— B to — E	..	..	..	..	..	*ea*		3·00	2·00
— H		..	..	..	..	..		3·00	2·00
— J to — N	..	..	..	..	..	*ea*		3·00	2·00
— R		..	..	..	..	..		8·50	3·00

B297 obverse
Queen's portrait

B297 reverse
Child Britannia

B297 **£5 blue** L No. No.

A	—	..	..	..	..	..	..	12·00	7·50
B	— to E —	..	..	..	..	.. ea	8·50	7·00
H	—	..	..	..	..	..	..	8·50	7·00
J	— to L —	..	..	..	..	.. ea	8·50	7·00
N	—	..	..	..	..	..	..	8·50	7·00
R	—	..	..	..	..	..	..	10·00	7·50

B299 obverse
Queen's portrait

41

B299 reverse
Lion, key & scroll

1964							EF	VF
B299	**£10 brown**	L No. No.						
	A —	..	..	..	..	..	18·00	13·00

SIGNATURE J. S. FFORDE
Chief Cashier 1966-70

B301, 305 obverse
Queen's portrait

B301, 305 reverse
Seated Britannia

1967   EF   VF

B301   **£1 green**   L No. No. L

		EF	VF
B — Y		8·00	4·00
C — Y or D — Y	ea	4·00	2·50
H — Y		4·00	2·50
J — Y to L — Y	ea	4·00	2·50
A — Z to E — Z	ea	4·00	2·50
H — Z		4·00	2·50
J — Z or L — Z	ea	4·00	2·50

See also B305.

"G" variety on reverse

43

B303 **£1 green** L No. No. L, with capital "G" on reverse

E — Y	.. ..	6·00	3·00
K — Z	.. ..	6·00	3·00

The "G" identified printing on a Gobel machine. *See also* B307.

B305 **£1 green** L No. No. L

N — A	.. ..	3·50	2·00
N — B to N — E	.. .. *ea*	3·00	2·00
N — H	.. ..	3·00	2·00
N — J to N — L	.. .. .. *ea*	3·00	2·00
R — A	.. ..	3·00	2·00
R — C to R — E	.. .. .. *ea*	3·00	2·00
R — H	.. ..	3·00	2·00
R — J or R — K	.. .. .. *ea*	3·00	2·00
S — A to S — E	.. .. .. *ea*	3·00	2·00
S — H	.. ..	3·00	2·00
S — J to S — L	.. .. .. *ea*	3·00	2·00
T — A to T — E	.. .. .. *ea*	3·00	2·00
T — H	.. ..	3·00	2·00
T — J to T — L	.. .. .. *ea*	3·00	2·00
U — A to U — D	.. .. .. *ea*	3·00	2·00
W — A to W — C	.. .. .. *ea*	3·00	2·00
X — B or X — C	.. .. .. *ea*	3·00	2·00

B307 **£1 green** L No. No. L with capital "G" on reverse

R — B	.. ..	5·00	2·50
R — L	.. ..	5·00	2·50
U — E	.. ..	5·00	2·50

The "G" identified printing on a Gobel machine.

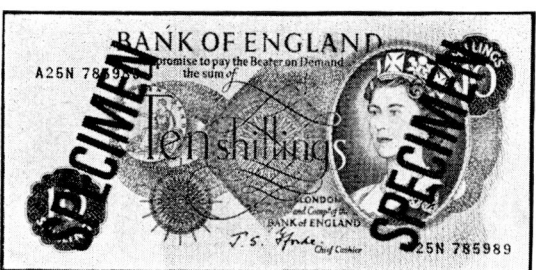

B310 obverse
Queen's portrait

B309/10 reverse
Seated Britannia

B309	**10s. red-brown**	No. No. L							
	— R	..	..	..	..	..	..	5·00	2·00
	— S to — U	..	..	..	..	.. ea	3·00	1·50
	— W to — Y	..	..	..	..	.. ea	3·00	1·50
	— Z	..	..	..	..	..	..	4·50	2·00

B310	**10s. red-brown**	L No. No. L						
	A — N	..	..	..	..	..	..	3·00	1·50
	B — N to D — N	..	..	..	..	3·00	1·50

B314 obverse
Queen's portrait

B312/14 reverse
Child Britannia

B312 **£5 blue** L No. No.

R —		..	..	..	..	..		10·00	7·50
S — to U —	..	..	..	..	..	..	*ea*	8·50	7·00
W — to Z —	..	..	..	..	..	..	*ea*	8·50	7·00

B314 **£5 blue** No. No. L

— A		..	..	..	..	..		9·00	7·00
— B to — E	..	..	..	..	..	..	*ea*	8·00	7·00
— H		..	..	..	..	..		8·00	7·00
— J to — L	..	..	..	..	..	..	*ea*	8·00	7·00

B316 obverse
Queen's portrait

B316 reverse
Lion, key & scroll

B316 **£10 brown** L No. No.

    A —   ..   ..   16·50   12·00

B318 obverse
Queen's portrait

B318 reverse
Shakespeare

							EF	VF
1970								
B318	**£20 multicoloured** (purple predominating) L No. No.							
	A —	..	..	..	..	..	30·00	25·00

SIGNATURE J. B. PAGE
Chief Cashier from 1970

PORTRAIT SERIES

B320 obverse
Queen's portrait

B320/2 reverse
Seated Britannia

1971								EF	VF
B320	**£1 green**	L No. No. L							
	S — L	..	..	..	..	..	..	10·00	4·00
	T — B	..	..	..	..	..	..	2·00	†
	T — D or T — E	..	..	..	..	ea	2·00	†
	T — H	..	..	..	..	..	..	2·00	†
	T — K or T — L	..	..	..	..	ea	2·00	†

U — A to U — D ..	..	..	..	*ea*	2·00	†
U — H	..	..	..		2·00	†
W — A to W — E ..	..	..	..	*ea*	2·00	†
W — H	..	..	..		2·00	†
X — A to X — E ..	..	..	..	*ea*	2·00	†
X — H	..	..	..		2·00	†
X — J to X — L ..	..	..	..	*ea*	2·00	†
Y — A to Y — E ..	..	..	..	*ea*	2·00	†
Y — H	..	..	..		2·00	†
Y — J to Y — L ..	..	..	..	*ea*	2·00	†
Z — A to Z — E ..	..	..	..	*ea*	2·00	†
Z — H	..	..	..		2·00	†
Z — J to Z — L ..	..	..	..	*ea*	2·00	†

B322 **£1 green** L L No. No.

AN — or BN —	..	..	...	..	*ea*	2·50	†
AR — or BR —	..	..	..	..	*ea*	2·00	†
AS — or BS —	..	..	..	..	*ea*	2·00	†
AT — or BT —	..	..	..	..	*ea*	2·00	†
AU — or BU —	..	..	..	..	*ea*	2·00	†
AW — or BW —	..	..	..	..	*ea*	2·00	†
AX — or BX —	..	..	..	..	*ea*	2·00	†

B324 obverse
Queen's portrait

B324 reverse
Child Britannia

B324 **£5 blue**   No. No. L
— C to — E	..	..	..	..	.. *ea*	8·00	6·50
— H ·	..	..	..	..	..	8·00	6·50
— J to — L	..	..	..	..	.. *ea*	8·00	6·50

B326 obverse
Queen's portrait

B326 reverse
Lion, key & scroll

B326 **£10 brown** L No. No.
B — to D — .. .. *ea* 15·00 12·00

PICTORIAL SERIES

B328 obverse
Queen's portrait

B328 reverse
Shakespeare

1970

								EF	VF
B328	**£20 multicoloured** (purple predominating)						L No.	No.	
A —	..	..	..	..	..	..		25·00	†
B — or C —	..	..	..	..	*ea*	22·00			†

B330 obverse
Queen's portrait

B330 reverse
Florence Nightingale

1975   EF   VF

B330   **£10 multicoloured** (brown predominating)   L No. No.

A —   ..   ..   12·00   †

B332 obverse
Queen's portrait

B332 reverse
Duke of Wellington

1971   EF   VF

B332 **£5 multicoloured** (pale blue predominating) L No. No.

A —	..	..	..	..	..	..	7·50	†
B — to E —	..	..	..	..	.. ea	6·00	†
H —	..	..	..	..	..	..	6·00	†
J — to L —	..	..	..	..	.. ea	6·00	†

"L" variety on reverse

1973   EF   VF

B334 **£5 multicoloured** (pale blue predominating) No. No. L

— A to — E	..	..	..	..	.. ea	6·00	†
— H	..	..	..	..	..	6·00	†
— J to — L	..	..	..	..	.. ea	6·00	†

The "L" signifies lithographic printing.
Note also serial prefix differs from B332.

Forming a Collection

Don't be too concerned about obtaining older notes in perfect condition. Only a handful of perfect Bank of England notes, issued up to the turn of the century, now exist, and these notes are acceptable in almost any condition. Naturally, modern notes should be collected in at least EF (extremely fine) condition where possible. However, this is not always possible and many notaphilists are happy to put aside VF (very fine) notes of, say, Hollom from circulation, which although recent are already scarce, replacing them with better examples when they come along.

Badly creased and dirty notes can benefit by soaking and then pressing them between heavy books, but generally speaking it is better, as with stamps, to leave them alone; cleaning with washing-up liquids, etc., adversely affects the notaphilic value, while ironing produces an artificial sheen which destroys much of their value to the collector.

Notes can be mounted in specially made albums (including the Stanley Gibbons). A type that has much to recommend it is the Hagner; this album has its pages already divided to accommodate the usual sizes of English notes. The pockets of crystal clear sheeting contain black card, which enhances the appearance of the notes, and are open at the top. Many collectors prefer this type to the floppy vinyl pockets opening from the side which are used by other makers.

There are many ways of forming a collection, ranging from the "one of each" type of collection to specialisation in low serial numbers—particularly the "A" series (A01A 000001), same number serials (M23L 555555), and one of each serial prefix of a particular Cashier, i.e. A...; B..., C..., D... etc.

Forgeries

It is an offence for anyone to purchase, receive from any person, or have in his custody or possession a forged banknote knowing it to be forged regardless of its age or country of origin. Forged notes are, in fact, immediately confiscated. **It is also illegal to photograph or photocopy a Bank of England note without the express authority of the Bank of England.**

Replacement Notes

A replacement note is used by the Bank of England to make up a bundle where one or more notes may have been damaged. At various points in the production run, a note from a bundle bearing a different serial prefix from the series in progress is inserted. As printing has become more highly complex, so the rate of faulty notes has increased, but even so it is still a minute fraction of the total.

Only the Bank of England can positively identify a replacement note, but although most of the replacement serials are now known, it is essential with present-day issues to preserve the note buttressed on each side by notes from from the normal series. This is because replacement serials are often released in blocks for general circulation, especially at the end of a run.

The following serial prefixes are known to have been used for replacements:

Cashier	10s.	£1	£1 ("G" reverse)
K. O. Peppiatt (threaded)	—A	S—S	
P. S. Beale	—A	S—S	
L. K. O'Brien	—A	S—S	
		S—T	
L. K. O'Brien (portrait)	M—	M—	
J. Q. Hollom	M—	M—	M—N
		—M	
		M—R	
J. S. Fforde	M—	M—R	M—N
		R—M	N—M
		S—M	T—M
		T—M	
		U—M	
J. B. Page		R—M	
		S—M	
		W—M	
		X—M	
		MR—	
		MS—	

All higher denomination notes in the portrait series are replaced by notes with the prefix M— (and in the case of Fforde and Page £5 notes by —M also).

Opinion is divided as to the existence of a recognisable replacement system before the Second World War. Nothing has come to light to prove or disprove the various serial letters suggested, and the Bank of England are not prepared to confirm or deny the existence of replacement notes during this period.

In Treasury notes, the odd letter out is Z, which was used to prefix the bottom right-hand note of each sheet of £1 notes (but not 10s. notes) from the Third Issue onwards. While Z prefix notes of Bradbury and Fisher are therefore slightly more rare, there is nothing to suggest they were deliberately set aside as replacements and may have acted rather as "control" notes.

Errors and Specimens

With the exception of the modern portrait £1 notes of Fforde and Page, and the £5 Wellington notes, errors are relatively scarce and in pre-war Bank of England and Treasury notes extremely rare. Because of this it is difficult to put an exact price on every single type of error that can occur.

However, the following classification deals with most of the relevant errors, and a *minimum* price is quoted (i.e. that which might be asked for a modern portrait note). As a rough guide, collectors should expect to pay double these prices for errors on post-war Britannia notes, a premium of 50% for pre-war notes and treble the prices below for Treasury note errors (except specimens). The prices below are for 10s. and £1 notes only; higher denominations would be treated pro rata.

Conversely specimen notes are generally found only in the earlier notes, though any specimen is extremely rare. Modern Bank of England practice is to release photographs only of specimen notes.

For the purpose of quotation the original catalogue number together with the suffix should be cited:

A. Specimen notes, overprinted SPECIMEN and generally numbered A00 000000, Q00 000000 (wartime issues, or R00 000000 (post war Britannia notes)   from £125
B. Serial numbers missing top and bottom   from £25
C. One serial number missing (or partly missing)   from £15
D. Top serial number different from bottom (Portrait notes)   from £6
E. Identical serial numbers on a pair of notes from £15 the pair
F. Identical but different serial numbers top and bottom on a pair of notes   from £25 the pair
G. Note printed on one side only   from £20
H. Part of design omitted   from £10
J. Double or faulty printing   from £8
K. Extra paper, through faulty folding   from £10

Collectors are invited to submit details of any other type of error note in which they are specifically interested.